THE RULES
OF GOLF

according to
DENNiS the MENACE

GOLF
MENACE

DENNIS THE MENACE AND GNASHER

In 1951, the year Max Faulkner won the Open Championship at Royal Portrush, Dennis the Menace "teed off" as a half-page strip in *The Beano* – Britain's well-loved children's comic.

With hair like the wildest rough a golfer could imagine, Dennis has an appetite for mischief which would surely make him the number one Menace in the Sony World Rankings.

In 1968, the year before a Briton next won the Open, Dennis was joined by his now constant canine companion, Gnasher – a hound with teeth so powerful that he crunches the most durable golf balls as if they were peppermints.

Dennis is a recent and enthusiastic convert to the Royal and Ancient game, his Mum and Dad having generously presented him with a set of cut-down clubs.

Generous? Not at all – it's all a clever ruse to allow Dennis's parents a few hours of peace to calm their shattered nerves and clear up the wreckage caused by Dennis.

Dennis and Gnasher invite you to join them for a light-hearted look at the Rules of Golf – a unique chance to laugh and learn.

THE RULES
OF GOLF

according to
DENNIS the MENACE

with the *reluctant* approval of
THE ROYAL AND ANCIENT
GOLF CLUB OF ST. ANDREWS

MICHAEL JOSEPH
LONDON

MICHAEL JOSEPH LTD

Published by the Penguin Group
27 Wrights Lane, London W8 5TZ
Viking Penguin Inc., 375 Hudson Street, New York 10014, USA
Penguin Books Australia Ltd, Ringwood, Victoria, Australia
Penguin Books Canada Ltd., 10 Alcorn Avenue, Toronto, Ontario, Canada M4V 3B2
Penguin Books (NZ) Ltd., 182 – 190 Wairau Road, Auckland 10, New Zealand

Penguin Books Ltd., Registered Offices: Harmondsworth, Middlesex, England

First published in Great Britain 1994

Colour reproduction by
Anglia Graphics Ltd.

Printed and bound in Great Britain by
William Clowes Ltd, Beccles and London

ISBN 0 7181 3850 3

The moral right of the author has been asserted

CONTENTS

FORE!word

The game of golf is ever-growing in popularity around the world; in fact it is one of the fastest-growing participant sports, being taken up by many thousands of new players each year.

Among those many new golfers, it appears, is the famous mischief-maker from *The Beano* comic, Dennis the Menace. Golf is a game with many rules, customs and etiquette, however, and as his millions of fans across the generations know, Dennis has never been one to go by the rules!

He is a maker of mayhem, a causer of chaos wherever he goes. So when he, accompanied by Gnasher, his partner-in-mischief – and occasional caddie – take to the course, the result is likely to be outrage, alarm and even injury to his fellow golfers.

So why, you may ask, would the Royal and Ancient Golf Club of St. Andrews – 'Home of Golf' and source of the Rules – give its blessing (however 'reluctant'!) to such a work as *The Rules of Golf According to Dennis the Menace*?

Well, first and foremost, this book is intended as entertainment. The absurd juxtaposition of Dennis the Menace and the game of golf is the first stage of fun. The extraordinary ways that Dennis finds to flaunt, or even rewrite the rules, is the next stage.

His antics cap any golfer's tall story you may have heard on the Nineteenth Hole!

But, through the antics of Dennis, his faithful hound Gnasher, and also his long-time protagonists, Walter and the Softies, the attention of golfers – both old and new – is drawn to specific rules with which they should be familiar, as well as to some which they may not come across so often.

Accompanying the rules, the little anecdotes (true stories every one) from the annals of the Royal and Ancient game serve to show the kind of stuff 'real' golfers are made of. They also demonstrate that, no matter what kind of spot you might find yourself in out there on the course, someone, somewhere, some time has been in a worse one!

Finally, it is our hope that this book may contribute towards easing the path of new golfers on to the course and increasing enjoyment for existing players.

JOHN S. SCRIVENER,
Chairman
Rules of Golf Committee,
Royal & Ancient Golf Club
of St. Andrews

When Arnold Palmer's hooked second shot landed in a fork in a gum tree during the second round of the Masters tournament at Melbourne, Australia in 1964, Palmer climbed 20 feet up the tree, hit the ball 30 feet forward with a one iron, chipped on to the green and holed out with one putt.

Rule 1-2. Exerting Influence on Ball

No player or caddie shall take any action to influence the position or the movement of a ball, except in accordance with the Rules.

For a bet, John Ball attempted to go round Hoylake in dense fog in under two-and-a-quarter hours, scoring less than 90 and without losing a ball. He did it in 81 with time to spare.

If any point in dispute is not covered by the Rules, the decision shall be made in accordance with equity.

Dressed in a full suit of armour the late
Henry Dearth, a famous vocalist, was
beaten 2 and 1 in a match at Bushey
Hall in 1912.

In stroke play you must always hole out. In match play your opponent may concede your next stroke.

A scratch player and a high-handicap man played each other on level terms in a match in the south of England, the only stipulation being that the scratch man was to drink a whisky and soda on each tee. One hole in the lead, the scratch man collapsed on the 16th, the high-handicap man taking the match.

The club must have a shaft and head. It must be one fixed unit and must not be substantially different from the traditional and customary form and make.

As a charity stunt in 1961, four Aberdeen University students tried to golf their way up Britain's highest peak, 4,406 ft Ben Nevis. But after 63 lost balls and 659 strokes, they gave up.

Rule 4-1. Club Damage

If a player's club ceases to conform because of damage sustained in the normal course of play the player may, without unduly delaying play, repair it.

The first ever golf shots on the Moon's
surface were played by Captain Alan
Shepard, commander of Apollo 14, in
1971. He claimed 200 yards with his
first shot. His second was a shank.

A player is limited to a maximum of 14 clubs.

In 1955 a player on the Eden course at
St Andrews sliced his drive from the
first tee as a train was passing on the
nearby railway line. The ball went in
through an open window and, a few
seconds later, was thrown back on to
the fairway by a passenger.

Rule 5-2. Foreign Material

No foreign material shall be applied to the ball for the purpose of changing its playing characteristics… Penalty — disqualification.

During a 24-hour period in November 1971, non-golf-playing athlete Ian Colson played 401 holes over a course in Victoria, Australia. Using only a 6-iron, Colson was assisted by a team of runners who looked for his ball and light at night was provided by a team of motorcyclists.

Rule 5-3. Ball Unfit for Play

A ball is unfit for play if it is visibly cut, cracked or out of shape. A ball is not unfit for play solely because mud or other materials adhere to it, its surface is scratched or scraped or its paint is damaged or discoloured.

When a team of archers played a team of golfers over Kirkhill Course, Lanarkshire in 1953, the archers won by two games to one. An arrow landing six feet from the hole, or a ball three feet, were counted as holed. Archers whose arrows landed in bunkers lifted the arrow and added a stroke.

Rule 6-5. Ball

The responsibility for playing the proper ball rests with the player. Each player should put an identification mark on his ball.

During the 1922 Scottish Amateur
Championship, a player who was
noted for his slow play had a large
hint dropped upon him. In an attempt
to make the slow player speed up, his
opponent brought a camp bed to the
course. The bed was put down at the
side of each green, and while the slow
player dawdled about, his opponent
rested on the bed. This ploy was
unsuccessful — the slow player
slowed down even more.

Rule 6-7. Undue Delay

The player must play without undue delay.

In February, 1950, Max Faulkner and
his partner, R. Dolman, in a Guildford
Alliance event finished their round in
complete darkness. A photographer's
flash bulbs were used at the last hole
to direct Faulkner's approach. Several
others of more than 100 competitors
also finished in the darkness.

Rule 6-8. Discontinuance of Play

Bad weather is not of itself a good reason for discontinuing play.

Rule 8-1. Advice

A player shall not give advice to anyone in the competition except his partner. A player may ask for advice from only his partner or either of their caddies. (Information on the Rules is not considered to be advice.)

On the glorious 12th of August, the
opening of the grouse-shooting
season, an 11-year-old schoolboy
William Fraser of Kingussie, downed a
grouse with his shot on the local
course.

Rule 8-2. Indicating Line of Play

When the player's ball is on the putting green... no mark shall be placed anywhere to indicate a line for putting.

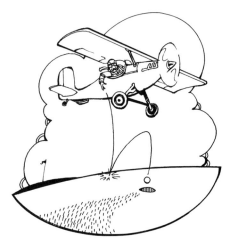

Golfing airman, Captain Pennington, once challenged professional A.J. Young to an air-versus-ground match. Pennington, who had 80 balls with him in his aircraft, had to circle over the course dropping his balls to land on the greens. Pennington took 29 "strokes" in a time of 40 minutes — Young took 68 in a time of 2 hours.

Rule 9-2. Information as to Strokes Taken

If asked, a player must tell his opponent how many strokes he has played.

Heavy rain on Rose Bay golf course,
New Zealand, in 1931 turned a bunker
into quicksand and a 14-stone golfer
who stepped unsuspectingly into it had
to be rescued as he sank to his
shoulders.

In searching for his ball anywhere on the course, the player may touch or bend long grass, rushes, bushes, whins, heather or the like, but only to the extent necessary to find and identify it, provided that this does not improve the lie of the ball, the area of his intended swing, or his line of play.

Although shut in for three years around the eternal snow and ice of the Antarctic, Arbroath golfer Munro Sievwright did not neglect his practice with club and ball. His luggage included three clubs and a dozen red-painted golf balls. In the light of the midnight sun he hit adventurous shots along the white wasteland on fairways on hard-packed snow.

Rule 13-1. Ball Played as it Lies

The ball shall be played as it lies, except as otherwise provided in the Rules.

F.G. Tait, at St Andrews, drove a ball
through a man's hat and had to pay
the owner 5/- (25p) to purchase a new
one. At the end of the round he was
grumbling to old Tom Morris about the
cost of this particular shot, when the
sage of St Andrews interrupted him,
"Eh, Mr Tait, you ought to be glad it
was only a new hat you had to buy,
and not an oak coffin."

Rule 13-3. Building a Stance

A player is entitled to place his feet firmly in taking his stance, but he must not build a stance.

Two players playing chip shots
simultaneously from opposite sides of
the fairway on the 9th at Wentworth
Falls in Australia were amazed to see
the balls hit each other in the air above
the green… and both fell into the hole!

Rule 16-1. Repair of Damage to Putting Green

The player may only repair a pitch mark or old hole plug on his line of putt.

Gerald Moxom came straight from a
wedding to play in the Captain's Prize
competition at West Hill, Surrey in
1934 and, dressed in complete
morning suit, went round in 71 to win
the competition.

Rule 17-1. The Flagstick

Before and during the stroke, the player may have the flagstick attended, removed or held up.

It took Floyd Rood 1 year and 114 days to golf his way from coast to coast across the U.S.A. The length of the 'course' was 3,397 miles for which Rood took 114,747 shots (including 3,511 penalty shots).

Rule 18-2. Ball Moving After Address

If a player's ball in play moves after he has addressed it, the player is deemed to have moved the ball and he incurs a penalty stroke.

On a damp and low-lying course a
player in a match watched in delight as
his 30-yard approach shot rolled
across the green and disappeared into
the hole. His delight changed into
disbelief when the ball popped back
out a couple of seconds later and a
frog jumped out of the hole.

Rule 19-1. Ball Deflected by Outside Agency

If a ball in motion is accidentally deflected or stopped by an outside agency, it is a rub of the green...and the ball shall be played as it lies.

A Brigadier Critchley travelled all the
way from New York to Southampton
and then flew to Sandwich to take part
in the Amateur Championship of 1937
and, despite flying over the clubhouse
to let the officials know he was there...
he was disqualified for being six
minutes late.

Rule 19-2. Ball Deflected by Player or Caddie

If a player's ball is accidentally deflected or stopped by himself, his partner or either of their caddies or equipment, he loses the hole in match play, or in stroke play he incurs a two-stroke penalty.

In Ireland's three-week national festival, An Tostal, in 1953, a cross country golf competition, was organised. The golfers played from the first tee of Kildare Club to the 18th green, five miles away, on the Curragh course. Hazards included a railway line, a main road, a racecourse and an army exercise area. The first competition was won by amateur internationalist, Joe Carr, with a score of 52!

Rule 21. Cleaning Ball

A ball on the putting green may be cleaned when lifted.

One of the players in the English Open Amateur Stroke Play at Moortown in 1971 overhit his shot to the last green and the ball bounced up the steps into the clubhouse, coming to rest in the bar. The clubhouse was not out of bounds, so the player opened a window and chipped through it on to the green.

Rule 23-1. Loose Impediments

Loose impediments — natural objects such as stones which are not fixed or solidly embedded — may be removed without penalty.

Casual water is any temporary accumulation of water on the course but not in a water hazard.

A player once hit a ball towards the
16th green of Combe Wood Golf Club,
and the ball landed in the vertical
exhaust pipe of a moving tractor. This
created a temporary loss of power in
the tractor, but when enough
compression had built up in the
exhaust pipe, the ball was forced out
at great speed and eventually landed 3
feet from the pin!

A ball is "lost" if it is not found or identified within five minutes...

In 1929, a husband and wife, whose
house was close to a fairway of a
course in Hampshire, were shocked
when a golf ball came rattling down the
chimney and landed in the fire. A
player's high tee shot had flown out of
bounds and the ball had popped
perfectly into the chimney pot.

Rule 27-2. Provisional Ball

If a ball may be lost outside a water hazard or be out of bounds, to save time, the player may play another ball provisionally as nearly as possible at the spot from which the original ball was played.

At Arizona's Glen Canyon course, a
local rule states — "If your ball lands
within one club's length of a
rattlesnake, you may move the ball."

Rule 28. Ball Unplayable

The player is the sole judge as to whether his ball is unplayable.

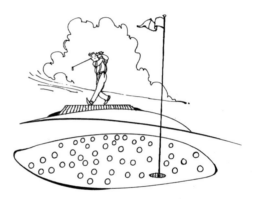

American professional, Harry Gonder, hit 1817 balls over a 16-hour 25-minute period at a 160-yard hole, trying for a hole-in-one. The closest he came to success was hitting the pin once.

Rule 34-2. Referee's Decisions

If a referee has been appointed by the Committee, his decision is final.

In 1907 during a Medal meeting of the Royal and Ancient at St. Andrews, a member's tee shot struck the sharp point of a pin in the hat of a lady who was crossing the course. The lady was not hurt, and the ball was firmly impaled.

Moving a rattling or squeaking cart while an opponent plays a stroke is poor sportsmanship.

In one of the rounds of the News Of
The World Matchplay Championship in
1960, W.S. Collins and W.J. Branch
were all-square after 18 holes... and it
took till the 31st hole to decide the
match, Collins winning. In 1961 in the
same tournament, Harold Henning
took 31 holes to beat Peter Alliss in the
third round.

Do not drop your golf bag, clubs or any equipment on the putting green.

In a match in 1921 at Kirkfield, Ontario, P. McGregor needed a long putt on the last green to win. His ball rolled up to the lip of the hole and stopped… then a grasshopper landed on the ball and it fell into the hole!

Never step on the line of another player's putt.

When Abe Mitchell and John Ball were playing in the last round of the final of the Amateur Championship at Westward Ho! in 1912, Mitchell's drive to the short 14th hit the open umbrella of a woman spectator and bounced into a bunker. Mitchell was 2 holes up at the time, but lost that hole — eventually the Championship, too, at the 38th.

Etiquette. While a Stroke is Being Played

You should not move, talk, or stand close to or directly behind a player making a stroke.

In a match at Esher in 1931, the club professional, George Ashdown, played each of his shots from a rubber tee strapped to the forehead of Miss Ena Shaw!

No comment should be made to an opponent about his swing during a match.

Spotting a 95-year-old member
slumped in a golf-buggy at Point Grey
Golf Club, Vancouver, a golfer asked
what was wrong. "Heart failure," he
thought the old man said — so he
dashed to the clubhouse to call an
ambulance. Much to the golfer's
embarrassment, there was nothing
wrong with the old man. It turned out
that he had said "Cart failure —!"

Local Rules governing the use of golf carts must be strictly observed.

Tuctu Golf Club in Peru is thought to be the highest in the world, at 14,335 feet. Bolivia boasts one at 13,500 feet — the La Paz Golf Club.

Etiquette. Opponent Driving Off

When your opponent is driving off you should stand where he can see you, but do not stand behind a player, or in such a position that he may be distracted.

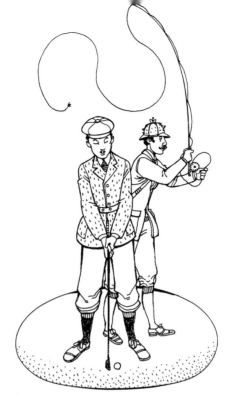

In 1913, at Wellington, Shropshire, a match between a golfer and a fisherman casting a 2½ oz. weight was played. The golfer, Rupert May, took 87, the fisherman, JJD Mackinlay, required 102. The fisherman's difficulty was in his short casts. His longest cast, 105 yards, was within 12 yards of the world record at the time. When within a rod's length of a hole, he ran the weight to the rod end and dropped into the hole. Five times he broke the line, and was allowed another shot without penalty.

Always play without undue delay and leave the putting green as soon as all the players in your group have holed out.

A ball driven off at the John O'Gaunt Club, Sutton, Bedfordshire, landed in London, 40 miles away! The ball actually landed in a passing vegetable lorry…and stayed there till it dropped out when the vegetables were being delivered to Covent Garden market in London.

Etiquette. Replacing Divots

Carefully replace any divots and smooth out footprints in bunkers.

In 1957 on Killarney golf course, a
player sliced his ball into a lake… and
it knocked out a fat trout rising to catch
a fly. The player's partner waded in to
retrieve the ball — and the trout!

Etiquette. The Flagstick

Always replace the flagstick carefully in the hole in an upright position.

Is there nowhere that golf cannot be
played? A Scottish enthusiast formed
the Polar Bear Club in the Arctic,
beating out a rough course in the snow
and ice, and local Eskimos were
among the membership.

Never hold up the players behind you. Invite faster groups to play through.

Finding his ball buried in a grassy
bunker at Hale, Cheshire, in 1935,
A.M. Chevalier played with a
niblick...and three balls came shooting
out, only for all of them to fall back into
the bunker, coming to rest within a foot
of each other.

Do not play your ball until any players ahead of you have moved out of range of your shot.

In the last Open Championship to be played at Musselburgh, near Edinburgh, in 1889, many players still had not completed their final rounds as night began to fall. Players who were not seriously in contention were paid to withdraw to speed up play and allow those with a chance to finish before it got dark.

Etiquette. The Last Putt

Every player should remain in or around the green until the last putt has dropped, before moving on to the next tee.

In 1938 at Downfield Golf Club,
Dundee, a golfer was about to play a
stroke when a minor whirlwind struck.
It blew his ball away, spun the player
round and whisked skywards a
wooden shelter which landed in
smithereens on the 11th green.

You should always leave the golf course in the condition in which you expect to find it.

AND FINALLY...

Me and Gnasher have had loads of laughs showing you how **NOT** to play golf.

OK, we got most of the Rules wrong first time, but now we've got the hang of them we'll stick to the right way from now on.

Menaces always play fair 'n' square, you know. It's best to stick to the Rules.

Got to go now – I'm teeing off against Desperate Dan from The Dandy in ten minutes.

Fetch my crash helmet, Gnasher – that cowboy's one wild hitter...

A copy of the Rules of Golf can be obtained from your club secretary or by sending a stamped addressed envelope to:-
Royal Insurance, Freepost (LV 7075), P.O. Box 144, Liverpool L69 4HQ.